The steadfast love of the LORD never ceases; his mercies never come to an end; they are new every morning; great is your faithfulness.

Lamentations 3:22-23
ESV

*Describe a "new morning" moment in your life—
a time when God gave you a fresh start.*

*What can you rejoice in today,
even if your circumstances aren't perfect?*

*How has God prepared you for this present moment?
Where do you see God's hand preparing you for the future?*

Reflect on a time God carried you through a difficult season. How did your faith grow during that experience?

"For nothing will be impossible with God."

Luke 1:37 ESV

What truths from God's Word do you need to speak to yourself today?

In what areas of your life is God calling you to trust Him more deeply?

How can you draw nearer to God in this season of life?

How can you create more stillness in your life?

This is the day that the LORD has made; let us rejoice and be glad in it.

— Psalm 118:24
ESV

Describe a time when God answered a prayer in a way you didn't expect.

List ten things you are thankful for today, no matter how small.

Reflect on something in nature that made you pause and thank God.

Describe a moment recently when you felt deeply grateful.

I can do all things through Christ who strengthens me.

Philippians 4:13
NKJV

Write about a recent blessing that reminded you of God's faithfulness.

What practices or habits could help you stay spiritually grounded?

In what ways do you see yourself growing into the woman God created you to be?

What dreams or passions has God placed in your heart for this season?

She is clothed with strength and dignity; she can laugh at the days to come.

Proverbs 31:25
NIV

*How do you define your purpose in this stage of life?
How can God use you now?*

Reflect on how your identity in Christ has changed the way you see yourself.

How can you share the beauty of Christ's love with the people around you?

What hurt or burden are you ready to release to God today?

"'Love the Lord your God with all your heart and with all your soul and with all your mind and with all your strength.'"

— Mark 12:30 NIV

Write a prayer for healing—physical, emotional, or spiritual.

*How have you forgiven yourself for past mistakes?
What does God say about forgiveness?*

Reflect on a time you experienced God's peace that passes all understanding.

How can you be a source of encouragement to another woman this week?

"Be strong and courageous. Do not be afraid; do not be discouraged, for the LORD your God will be with you wherever you go."

Joshua 1:9
NIV

*What role do you play in your family,
and how does God strengthen you in that role?*

Describe a friendship that has enriched your faith.

How can you cultivate more meaningful connections with others?

Who needs your prayers today?
Write out a prayer for them.

Faith is the assurance of things hoped for, the conviction of things not seen.

— Hebrews 11:1 ESV

What does hope mean to you today, and how does God renew your hope?

What has been one of the most spiritually defining moments of your life?

Who in your life helps you stay mindful of God's presence, and how do they inspire you?

What Bible verse helps you refocus on God throughout the day?

Those who hope
in the LORD
will renew their strength.
They will soar on
wings like eagles.

Isaiah 40:31
NIV

How have you seen God's promises come true in your life?

If you could share one piece of wisdom with your younger self, what would it be?

How have you grown closer to God in the past year?

*What part of God's character are you most thankful for—
His mercy, His love, His faithfulness, His forgiveness?*

Rejoice in the Lord always. I will say it again: Rejoice!

— Philippians 4:4 NIV

Where did you notice God's presence today, even in something small or ordinary?

What do you want future generations to remember most about your faith?

How has the faith of the women in your family influenced your walk with the Lord?

How does knowing that you are part of God's larger story inspire you to live today with purpose?

New Every Morning

Published by Guideposts

100 Reserve Rd., Suite E200

Danbury, CT 06810

Guideposts.org

Copyright © 2025 by Guideposts. All rights reserved.

This book, or parts thereof, may not be reproduced, stored in a retrieval system, or transmitted in any form or by any means, electronic, mechanical, photocopying, recording, or otherwise, without the written permission of the publisher.

To shop our best sellers and favorites, visit guideposts.org/shop.

Every attempt has been made to credit the sources of copyrighted material used in this book. If any such acknowledgment has been inadvertently omitted or miscredited, receipt of such information would be appreciated.

Scripture quotations marked (ESV) are taken from *The Holy Bible, English Standard Version*. Copyright © 2001 by Crossway Bibles, a division of Good News Publishers. Used by permission. All rights reserved.

Scripture quotations marked (NIV) are taken from *The Holy Bible, New International Version*. Copyright © 1973, 1978, 1984, 2011 by Biblica, Inc. Used by permission of Zondervan. All rights reserved worldwide. zondervan.com

Scripture quotations marked (NKJV) are taken from *The Holy Bible, New King James Version*. Copyright © 1982 by Thomas Nelson.

Cover and interior design by Juicebox Designs

Hand-lettering and illustration by Kristi Smith

ISBN 978-1-965859-39-1

Printed and bound in China